# HOMOGRAPHIC HOMOPHONES

fly and fly and other WORDS THAT LOOK AND SOUND THE SAME but are as different in meaning as bat and bat

# HOMOGRAPHIC HOMOPHONES

ILLUSTRATED BY JOAN HANSON

Published by
**Lerner Publications Company**
Minneapolis, Minnesota

for Judy

All rights reserved. International copyright secured. Manufactured
in the United States of America. Published simultaneously in Canada
by J. M. Dent & Sons Ltd., Don Mills, Ontario.

International Standard Book Number: 0-8225-0288-7
Library of Congress Catalog Card Number: 73-11973

**homographic homophone**   (HAHM-uh-graf-ick HAHM-uh-fone) A word that is spelled and pronounced the same as another word but has a different meaning. These words are homographic homophones: *bank* and *bank* (a river bank; money in the bank); *row* and *row* (row a boat; stand in a row).

**Row**

# Row

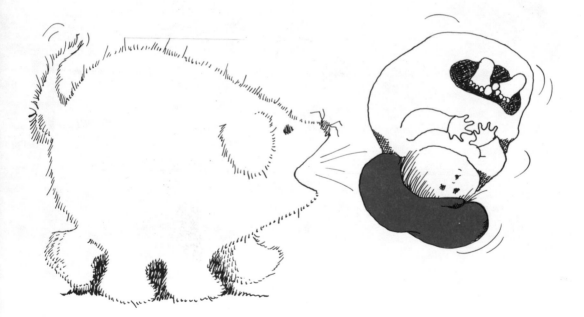

**Bark**

**Bark**

**Bat**

# Bat

**Scale**

**Scale**

**Ring**

**Ring**

**Bank**

Bank

**Bill**

**Bill**

**Box**

**Box**

**Pit**

**Pit**

**Rock**

**Rock**

**Batter**

**Batter**

**Fly**

**Fly**

**Toast**

**Toast**

# BOOKS IN THIS SERIES

## ANTONYMS
hot and cold and other
WORDS THAT ARE DIFFERENT
as night and day

## MORE ANTONYMS
wild and tame and other
WORDS THAT ARE AS DIFFERENT IN MEANING
as work and play

## HOMONYMS
hair and hare and other
WORDS THAT SOUND THE SAME
but look as different as bear and bare

## MORE HOMONYMS
steak and stake and other
WORDS THAT SOUND THE SAME
but look as different as chili and chilly

## HOMOGRAPHS
bow and bow and other
WORDS THAT LOOK THE SAME
but sound as different as sow and sow

## HOMOGRAPHIC HOMOPHONES
fly and fly and other
WORDS THAT LOOK AND SOUND THE SAME
but are as different in meaning as bat and bat

## British-American SYNONYMS
french fries and chips and other
WORDS THAT MEAN THE SAME THING
but look and sound
as different as truck and lorry

## MORE SYNONYMS
shout and yell and other
WORDS THAT MEAN THE SAME THING
but look and sound
as different as loud and noisy

*We specialize in producing quality books for*
*young people. For a complete list please write*

## LERNER PUBLICATIONS COMPANY
*241 First Avenue North, Minneapolis, Minnesota 55401*